Wolf Family
Adventures

Bobbie Kalman
Crabtree Publishing Company
www.crabtreebooks.com

Animal Family ADVENTURES

Created by Bobbie Kalman

Dedicated by Samantha Crabtree
For Lindsay's fierce little pack—
Shyler, Ethan, and Hayden Taylor!

Author
Bobbie Kalman

Photo research
Bobbie Kalman

Editors
Kathy Middleton
Crystal Sikkens

Design
Bobbie Kalman
Katherine Berti

Print and production coordinator
Katherine Berti

Photographs
Bigstockphoto: page 29 (bottom)
Dreamstime: page 28 (bottom right)
Superstock: Minden Pictures: page 4;
    Patrick Endres/ Alaska Stock - Design Pics:
    page 23
Thinkstock: pages 13 (bottom), 19 (bottom),
    25, 29 (middle)
Cover and other images by Shutterstock

Library and Archives Canada Cataloguing in Publication

Kalman, Bobbie, author
        Wolf family adventures / Bobbie Kalman.

(Animal family adventures)
Includes index.
Issued in print and electronic formats.
ISBN 978-0-7787-2234-2 (bound).--ISBN 978-0-7787-2242-7
(paperback).--ISBN 978-1-4271-1715-1 (html)

        1. Wolves--Juvenile literature. 2. Wolves--Infancy--Juvenile
literature. I. Title.

QL737.C22K356 2016   j599.77   C2015-908702-3
                                             C2015-908703-1

Library of Congress Cataloging-in-Publication Data

CIP available at Library of Congress

Crabtree Publishing Company
www.crabtreebooks.com   1-800-387-7650

Printed in Canada/052016/TL20160324

Published in Canada
Crabtree Publishing
616 Welland Ave.
St. Catharines, Ontario
L2M 5V6

Published in the United States
Crabtree Publishing
PMB 59051
350 Fifth Avenue, 59th Floor
New York, New York 10118

Published in the United Kingdom
Crabtree Publishing
Maritime House
Basin Road North, Hove
BN41 1WR

Published in Australia
Crabtree Publishing
3 Charles Street
Coburg North
VIC 3058

What is in this book?

Meet the wolf pups!

It is spring, and a gray wolf mother has just given birth to four pups in a big hole under the ground, known as a **nursery den**. The pups are covered in black fur. They are deaf, and their blue eyes are shut. They snuggle up to their mother, Olivia. We will call the pups Lilla, Joel, Timmy, and Eva.

Olivia takes care of her pups while they spend their first weeks sleeping. Other wolves in their family bring Olivia food while she is in the den with her pups. Wolves are animals called **mammals**. Mammal mothers **nurse**, or feed their babies milk made in their bodies. Olivia will nurse her pups until they are about two months old.

Part of a family

Pups are born into a wolf family called a **pack**. A pack is made up of parents and their young wolves. Larger packs also include aunts, uncles, brothers, sisters, and sometimes wolves from other packs. Members of a pack live together and work as a team to raise the younger wolves. They teach them how to hunt and how to survive in the wild. Only one male and one female in the pack make babies. They are called the alpha wolves. Olivia and Andy, the parents of the pups, are the alpha wolves of this pack.

The pack celebrated the birth of the pups by howling, racing around, and playing happily. Now, they look forward to helping Olivia take care of the pups and play with them. One female, Blanka, waits outside the den. She will help Olivia nurse the pups when they come out of the den in a few weeks.

Let's go outside!

The pups are now a month old, and they can't wait to come out of the den! They can see, hear, and walk, but the world outside is new to them, so they do not go very far. They have a lot to learn.

The wolves in the pack take turns watching the pups and keeping them safe. Timmy wonders how far down it is from the top of this rock. Should he jump? His father, Andy, is there to make sure his son doesn't get hurt.

Uncles and aunts

Uncle Leo watches the pups explore the forest.

They have found a dead log and are sniffing it.

Are there some insects inside or maybe a mouse?

Leo looks forward to teaching the pups how to hunt.

Aunt Blanka is like a second mother. She helps Olivia feed the pups and enjoys spending time with them. She plays with them and shows them love. Do you have an aunt that loves spending time with you? What kinds of things do you do together?

Animals in the forest

Gray wolf families live in many kinds of natural places, called **habitats**. Each wolf pack has a home area called a **territory**. A territory has fresh water and enough food for the pack. Other wolves know to stay away!

mouse

rabbit

deer with fawn

raccoon

chipmunk · squirrel

Other wolf packs do not live in Andy's territory, but his pack does share the forest with many kinds of animals. Rabbits, chipmunks, mice, squirrels, raccoons, and deer live in forests. Maybe the pups will even see a red fox hunting a rabbit in their forest home.

Grasses and flowers

At the edge of the forest where the pups live is a grassy area called a meadow. In spring, the meadow is filled with flowers. The pups enjoy playing there. Joel is jumping on Olivia's back, Lilla is smelling a flower, and Timmy is licking Olivia. Butterflies and honeybees fly above their heads, and grasshoppers jump between their legs. Suddenly, Eva spots her father at the edge of the forest.

Eva runs to greet Andy, who is sniffing a hole in the ground. They smell an animal down below. Could it be a rabbit? Many rabbits live in meadows.

First meat meals

Wolves are **carnivores**. Carnivores eat other animals. When the pups are a month old, they start eating meat. At first, they eat meat that adult wolves **regurgitate**, or bring up, from their stomachs. The pups look forward to these meals and race to be the first to get this meaty food. Andy, who just came back from hunting, opens his mouth to feed Joel, the first pup to greet Andy. The other pups see their father and run to get some meat, too.

When the pups are six weeks old, their family starts bringing them small animals that they can chew and eat themselves. Olivia has brought a rabbit. As adults, wolves eat mostly large animals such as deer, elk, and moose.

Playing and fighting

Olivia's pups spend most of their time playing. They leap and **pounce**, chase and wrestle, and play tag and hide-and-seek. They bite each other's necks and ears and push each other down on the ground.

Lilla is climbing up onto a rock, and Joel is running in the grass. The pups also play with bones, feathers, and the skins of dead animals that they find. They carry their toy "**prey**" around like trophies. Playing prepares them for hunting with their pack. Timmy and Eva are playing tug-of-war with a feather they found.

Time to leave the den

The pups have grown quickly. They are about two months old, and it is time to leave the den for good. They follow their pack to a meeting place in their territory. Every few weeks, the pack chooses a new meeting place.

Wolves gather at their meeting place to sleep, play, or just hang out with the pack. At three months, the pups start traveling with the pack on hunts, but they do not start hunting yet.

Hunting with the pack

Lilla, Joel, Timmy, and Eva are now eight months old. The pups look like adult wolves and are now ready to join the hunt. They **imitate** the older wolves and **cooperate** with one another while they hunt. Large animals such as deer and moose are hard to hunt and can take several days to bring down. One of these animals can feed many wolves.

The pack has been following a **herd** of moose for most of the day and have chosen which one they will hunt. Babies are usually the easiest to catch. This moose mother tried to keep her calf near her, but the wolves scared it away. It did not take the wolves long to catch the calf.

What did they say?

Animals that live in groups need to share information, or **communicate**, to let one another know what they are doing. Wolves howl, growl, whimper, and bark. They howl to let other wolves know where they are and to bring the pack together for a hunt. They also howl to warn other wolves to stay out of their territory and to celebrate the birth of pups. Whining and whimpering are sounds they make to show that they are happy to see one another.

Andy marks his territory with **urine**, or pee, which he sprays on trees. When other wolf packs smell the scent, they know they need to stay out of that area.

Wolves also communicate with their tails. Andy holds his tail high to say, "I am the boss." The rest of the pack hold their tails low to say, "We know you are."

Wolves growl and bare their teeth when they are angry. Andy growls at another wolf and also shows that he is the boss of the pack by holding the wolf underneath him.

Which dog is which?

Wolves belong to the dog family. Foxes, coyotes, African wild dogs, jackals, hyenas, and pet dogs are other kinds of dogs. Wolves are the biggest. Dogs have four legs, a tail, and a snout, which includes their mouth and nose. Their bodies are covered with red, gray, black, brown, or white fur. Dogs can walk and run fast. Their feet have paws with claws. Many dog pups look alike. Which of these pups is not a wild dog?

gray wolf pup

German shepherd pup

red fox pup

Compare the colors, ears, and snouts of each of these pups. Which pup looks most like a wolf? Which pup has the biggest ears? Which has the smallest? Which pup's fur is different from the fur of the others?

hyena pup

African wild dog pup

coyote pup

jackal pup

Match them up!

The pictures on these pages will help you remember what you have learned about wolves in this book. Match the pictures to the information in the box on the next page. Did you get them all?

Match the pictures to this information.

1. Wolf pups start coming out of their den when they are four weeks old.
2. The alpha wolf is the leader of the pack and stands above the other wolves in the pack.
3. Pups show that they want food to eat by licking the mouths of adult wolves.
4. Wolves hunt large animals such as deer and moose.
5. Mothers and other pack members show their pups a lot of love.
6. Newborn wolf pups have brown fur and blue eyes.

Answers

1. F, 2. A, 3. C, 4. E, 5. B, 6. D, F

Big bad wolves?

There are many fairy tales and movies that make us think that wolves are very bad animals. *Little Red Riding Hood* and *The Three Little Pigs* are just two of these. Children have been told these stories for many years, and in many movies today, wolves are still "big and bad." People kill wolves because they are afraid of them, but wolves do not hurt or kill people. They stay away from them.

Learn more

Wolves are a very important part of nature. They are the only **predators** that are large enough to hunt big animals. Without wolves keeping their numbers down, elk and moose would eat too many plants and make it harder for trees to grow. Without trees, there would be fewer birds of all kinds. Wolves also keep animal herds healthy by hunting the sick and old animals in the herds. Learn more about wolves and write your own stories to help people better understand them.

Words to know

Note: Some boldfaced words are defined where they appear in the book.

carnivore (KAHR-nuh-vawr) noun
An animal that eats other animals

communicate (kuh-MYOO-ni-keyt) verb
To exchange feelings and thoughts through sounds, smells, or body language

cooperate (koh-OP-uh-reyt) verb
To work together with others

herd (hurd) noun A group of plant-eating animals with hoofs that live together

imitate (IM-i-teyt) verb To follow or copy the actions of others

mammal (MAM-uh-l) noun A warm-blooded animal that is covered in hair or fur and gives birth to live young

nursery den (NUR-suh-ree den) noun
A shelter used by animals, in which they give birth to babies and care for them

pounce (pouns) verb To spring or leap suddenly to catch prey

predator (PRED-uh-ter) noun An animal that hunts and eats other animals

prey (prey) noun An animal that is hunted and eaten by another animal

regurgitate (ri-GUR-ji-teyt) verb To bring up food or liquid from the stomach

A noun is a person, place, or thing. A verb is an action word that tells you what someone or something does.

Index